Where does your food come from?

Food Atlas

the
BIG
PICTURE

Sarah Levete

Published 2010 by
A&C Black Publishers Ltd.
36 Soho Square, London, W1D 3QY

www.acblack.com

ISBN HB 978-1-4081-2790-2
      PB 978-1-4081-3162-6

Text copyright © 2010 Sarah Levete

This book is produced using paper that is made from wood grown in managed, sustainable forests. It is natural, renewable and recyclable. The logging and manufacturing processes conform to the environmental regulations of the country of origin.

Produced for A&C Black by Calcium. www.calciumcreative.co.uk

Printed and bound in China by C&C Offset Printing Co.

All the internet addresses given in this book were correct at the time of going to press. The author and publishers regret any inconvenience caused if addresses have changed or sites have ceased to exist, but can accept no responsibility for any such changes.

Acknowledgements

The publishers would like to thank the following for their kind permission to reproduce their photographs:

Cover: Shutterstock: Paul Prescott (front), Kurt De Bruyn (back). **Pages:** Shutterstock: 2happy 20-21, 2009fotofriends 12-13, Bocky 2-3, 22-23, Bofotolux 6-7, Norman Chan 14-15, EtiAmmos 16-17, Fotokkden 10-11, 24, Sebastian Knight 20, Arnold John Labrentz 1, 18, Patrick Lecarpentier 10-11, Michael Ledray 4, Dmitry Naumov 4-5, Pincasso 18-19, Quayside 3, 6, Dr. Morley Read 15b, Ian Scott 13, Jose Ignacio Soto 9, Pozzo Di Borgo Thomas 17, Tomashko 21, Ingrid W 8-9, XuRa 15t, Yellowj 7, Zurijeta 14.

Contents

Our Food

Take a look at the food on your plate. Some of it probably travelled a long way before it reached you.

Planes and trains

The food you eat comes from all over the world. It is carried to shops by planes, boats, and lorries.

Where does the food you eat come from?

4

Finding food

You buy food in a shop, but some people don't have shops. They eat the plants and animals where they live.

Crunch!

Fruit and Veg

Fruit and vegetables come in all colours and shapes. They grow in many different places.

Hot sun, cool earth

Some fruits, such as sweet **mango**, grow quickly in the hot sun. Others, such as carrots, grow better under the cool earth.

Have you eaten funny-looking fruit and vegetables?

Stinging soup?

Nettles grow wild in the countryside. You can use them to make a tasty soup – and it won't sting!

Spikey fruit!

Super Seed

Lots of bread and cereals **are made from** wheat.

Growing fast

Wheat starts as a tiny seed and grows into a tall, golden plant.

Brrum!

Combine harvesters have huge **blades** to cut the wheat.

Harvest time

Wheat is cut down by **combine harvesters** when it is **ripe**. The **grain** from the wheat is made into food.

Blades

Animals Too

Lots of food comes from animals such as chickens, goats, and sheep.

Milkshakes and more

Milk comes from cows and goats. It is used to make cheese, butter, yoghurts, cream, and even milkshakes.

Snake pie

People in different parts of the world eat different animals. Some people in cold countries eat **reindeer**. In other countries people eat kangaroos or snakes.

We get most of our milk from cows.

Moooo!

11

Fish Food

Fish come in all shapes and sizes. People catch fish that swim in rivers, lakes, and seas.

Smells fishy

Fishing boats put the fish they catch into huge icy fridges to stop it going bad. Rotten fish smells and tastes horrible!

Fish face!

Cod is a large fish that is eaten all over the world.

Seaweed bread?

Seaweed isn't just eaten by fish. You can eat pasta and bread made from seaweed.

13

Sweet Stuff

Do you know where chocolate and sweets come from? They begin life as plants.

Chocolate beans

Chocolate comes from **cocoa** beans. The beans are cooked until they turn into a brown liquid – chocolate!

Yum!

Sugar juice

Sugar cane is a tall grass. The juice from the cane is boiled and cleaned. This turns it into sweet sugar.

Cocoa pods grow on cocoa trees in hot countries.

On the Farm

Some farms are like small gardens with a few animals. Other farms are huge.

Monster machines

Farmers on big farms often use huge machines such as tractors and combine harvesters.

In some countries, farmers work without big machines.

Just enough

Farmers on small farms often grow just enough to feed their family or neighbours.

On the Move

In rich countries, people often eat food that is grown far away.

Food on the move

Lots of the food we eat is grown in hot countries. It is picked, packed, and sent to shops all over the world.

In poor countries, people usually only buy food grown there.

Flying food

Bus and plane

Trucks carry bananas from the field to the airport. Aeroplanes then fly them to the countries they are sold in.

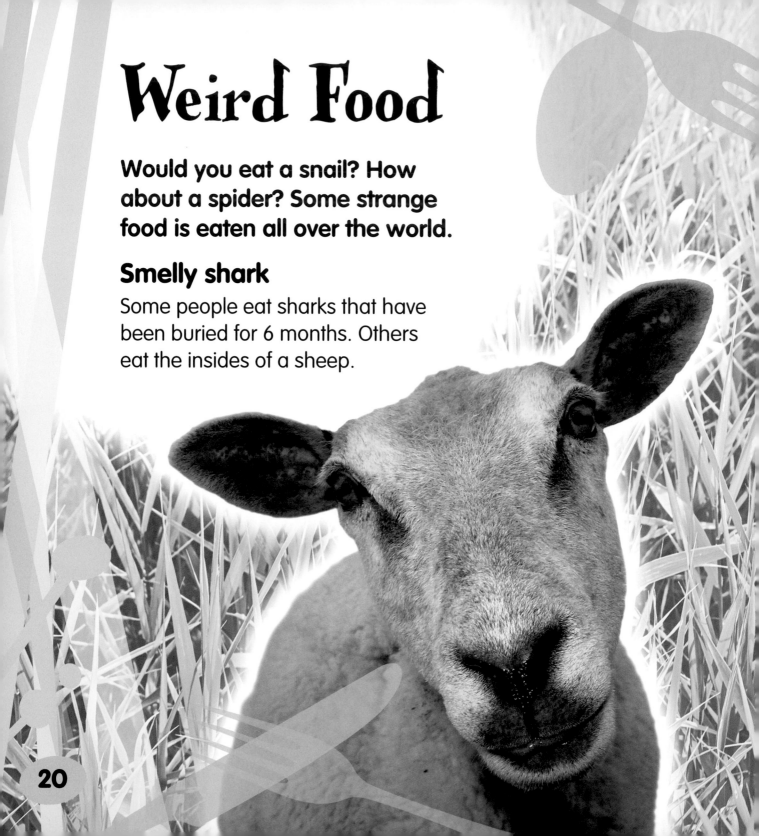

Weird Food

Would you eat a snail? How about a spider? Some strange food is eaten all over the world.

Smelly shark

Some people eat sharks that have been buried for 6 months. Others eat the insides of a sheep.

Tasty!

Spider snack

In some parts of the world, people eat giant crunchy spiders as a snack. Creepy!

Many people love to eat snails.

Glossary

blades sharp tools that can cut things

cereals grains that can be made into foods such as breakfast cereals, bread, and pasta

cocoa plant that contains beans from which chocolate can be made

cocoa pods part of the cocoa plant that contains cocoa beans

combine harvesters large machines that cut cereal plants when they are fully grown

grain seed-like part of a plant that is made into food

mango sweet, juicy fruit with an orange flesh

nettles green plants that can sting if touched

reindeer animals with long horns on their heads

ripe when a plant is ready to be eaten

seaweed slimy plant that grows in seawater

wheat cereal plant that is made into flour for foods such as bread, cakes, and pasta

Further Reading

Websites

Find out more about where food comes from at:
www.oxfam.org.uk/coolplanet/kidsweb/banana/ banana6.htm

See how a grain of wheat is turned into bread at:
www.grainchain.com

Books

Children and Their Food Around the World (Let's Eat!) by Beatrice Hollyer, Frances Lincoln (2005).

Food and Your World by Julia Allen and Margaret Iggulden, Franklin Watts (2008).

The Sun is a Cupcake and Other Poems About Food by Brian Moses, Wayland (2008).

Index